HAL•LEONARD

VIOLIN  PLAY-ALONG

VOL. 16

FOLK SONGS

ISBN 978-1-4234-8649-7

HAL•LEONARD®
CORPORATION
7777 W. BLUEMOUND RD. P.O. BOX 13819 MILWAUKEE, WI 53213

In Australia Contact:
Hal Leonard Australia Pty. Ltd.
4 Lentara Court
Cheltenham, 3192 Victoria, Australia
Email: ausadmin@halleonard.com.au

Jerry Loughney, Violin
Jon Peik, Banjo and Mandolin
Dan Maske, Keyboards, Percussion, Keyboard
Harmonica and Trumpet
Produced and Recorded by Dan Maske

Visit Hal Leonard Online at
www.halleonard.com

CONTENTS

Home on the Range

Lyrics by DR. BREWSTER HIGLEY
Music by DAN KELLY

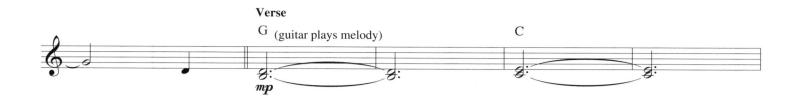

Verse

G (guitar plays melody)

C

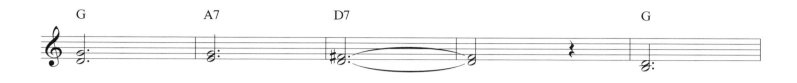

G　　　　A7　　　　D7　　　　　　　　　G

G7　　　　C　　　　Cm　　　　G/D　　　　D7

Chorus

G　　　　　　　　G　　　D7　　　G

G/B　　　A7　　　Am7　　　D7

G　　　　G7　　　C　　　Cm　　　G/D

D7　　　G　　　　　　　**Verse**

C　　　　　　　　　　G　　　A7　　　Am7

Chorus

Lyrics

1. Oh, give me a home where the buffalo roam,
   Where the deer and the antelope play,
   Where seldom is heard a discouraging word,
   And the skies are not cloudy all day.

   Chorus:
   Home, home on the range,
   Where the deer and the antelope play;
   Where seldom is heard a discouraging word,
   And the skies are not cloudy all day.

2. How often at night when the heavens are bright,
   From the light of the glittering stars,
   Have I stood there amazed and asked as I gazed,
   If their glory exceeds that of ours.
   Chorus

3. Where the air is so pure and the zephyrs so free,
   And the breezes so balmy and light;
   Oh, I would not exchange my home on the range
   For the glittering cities so bright.
   Chorus

4. Oh, give me a land where the bright diamond sand
   Flows leisurely down with the stream,
   Where the graceful white swan glides slowly along,
   Like a maid in a heavenly dream.
   Chorus

I've Been Working on the Railroad

American Folksong

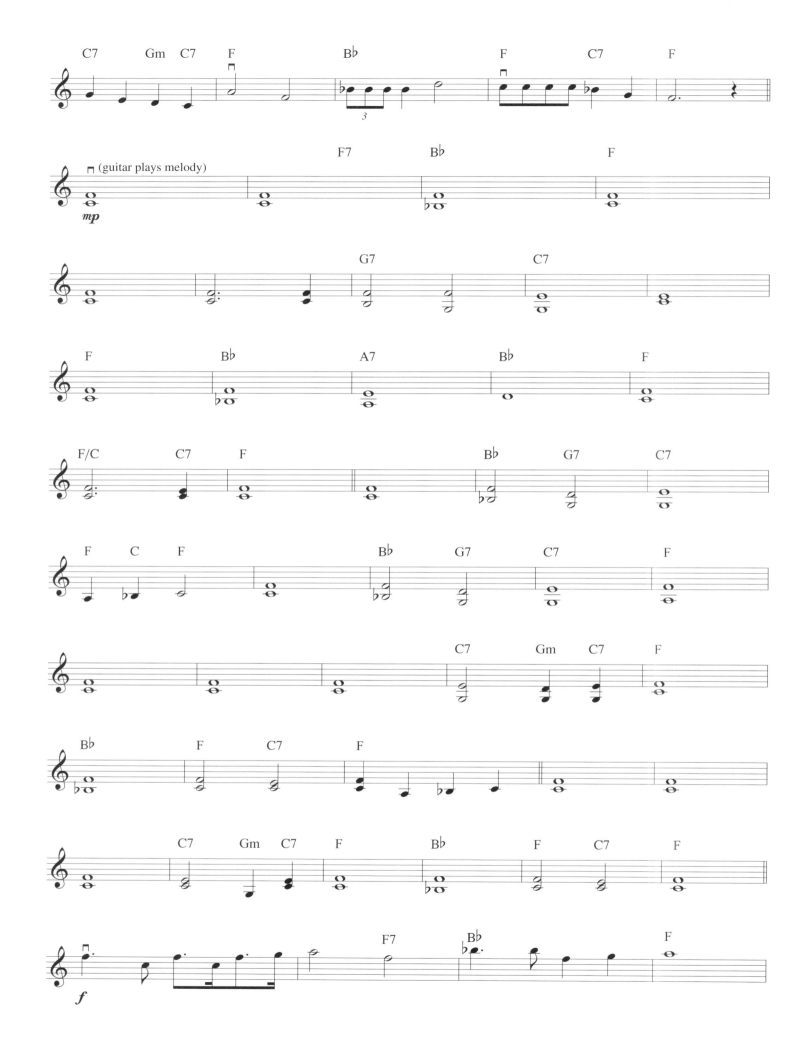

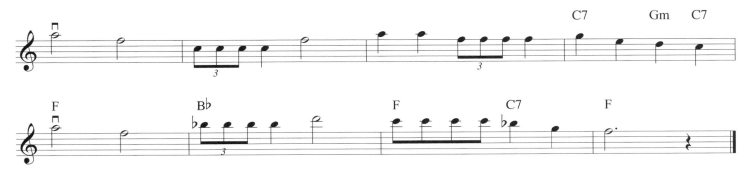

Lyrics

I've been working on the railroad, all the live long day.
I've been working on the railroad, just to pass the time away.
Can't you hear the whistle blowin'? Rise up so early in the morn.
Can't you hear the captain shoutin', "Dinah, blow your horn!"
Dinah, won't you blow, Dinah, won't you blow. Dinah, won't you blow your horn?
Dinah, won't you blow, Dinah, won't you blow, Dinah, won't you blow your horn?
Someone's in the kitchen with Dinah. Someone's in the kitchen I know.
Someone's in the kitchen with Dinah, strummin' on the old banjo and singin',
"Fee, fi, fiddle - ee - i - o, fee, fi, fiddle - ee - i - o.
Fee, fi, fiddle - ee - i - o," strummin' on the old banjo.

House of the Rising Sun

Southern American Folksong

Slowly and steadily

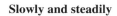

Lyrics

There is a house in New Orleans they call the Rising Sun.
And it's been the ruin of many a poor boy, and God, I know I'm one.

My mother was a tailor, sewed my new blue jeans.
My father was a gamblin' man down in New Orleans.
Now, the only thing a gambler needs is a suitcase and a trunk,
And the only time he'll be satisfied is when he's all a-drunk.

Oh! Mother, tell your children not to do what I have done:
Spend your lives in sin and misery in the house of the Rising Sun.
Well, I've got one foot on the platform, the other foot on the train.
I'm going back to New Orleans to wear that ball and chain.

Well, there is a house in New Orleans they call the Rising Sun.
And it's been the ruin of many a poor boy, and God, I know I'm one.

Midnight Special

Railroad Song

Lyrics

1. Wake up ev'ry morning,
   Same old atmosphere.
   Yearning for new places,
   Seems I like it anywhere but here.
   Let the Midnight Special shine her light on me.
   Let the Midnight Special shine her ever lovin' light on me.

2. Don't know where it's going,
   I don't even care.
   Any place it's going,
   Let her take me, let her take me there.
   Let the Midnight Special shine her light on me.
   Let the Midnight Special shine her ever lovin' light on me.

3. Don't we all get tired of the same routine?
   Longing for some somewhere,
   For a place that we have never seen.
   Let the Midnight Special shine her light on me.
   Let the Midnight Special shine her ever lovin' light on me.

Nobody Knows the Trouble I've Seen

African-American Spiritual

Lyrics

Nobody knows the trouble I've seen,
Nobody knows but Jesus!
Nobody knows the trouble I've seen,
Glory hallelujah!

Sometimes I'm feeling so far down,
Oh yes, Lord,
But my salvation can be found
In thee, dear Lord!

Oh! Nobody knows the trouble I've seen,
Nobody knows but Jesus!
Nobody knows the trouble I've seen,
Glory hallelujah!

When the Saints Go Marching In

Words by KATHERINE E. PURVIS
Music by JAMES M. BLACK

Lyrics

1. Oh, when the saints go marching in,
   Oh, when the saints go marching in,
   Oh Lord, I want to be in that number
   When the saints go marching in.

2. Oh, when the sun refuse to shine,
   Oh, when the sun refuse to shine,
   Oh Lord, I want to be in that number
   When the sun refuse to shine.

3. Oh, when they crown Him Lord of all,
   Oh, when they crown Him Lord of all,
   Oh Lord, I want to be in that number
   When they crown Him Lord of all.

4. Oh, when they gather 'round the throne,
   Oh, when they gather 'round the throne,
   Oh Lord, I want to be in that number
   When they gather 'round the throne.

Will the Circle Be Unbroken

Words by ADA R. HABERSHON
Music by CHARLES H. GABRIEL

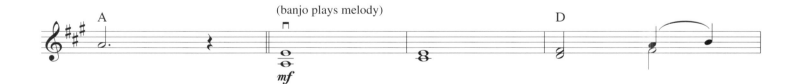

Lyrics

1. I was standing by my window,
   On one cold and cloudy day,
   When I saw the hearse come rolling,
   For to take my mother away.
   Will the circle be unbroken,
   By and by, Lord, by and by?
   There's a better home awaiting,
   In the sky, in the sky.

2. Oh, I told the undertaker,
   "Undertaker, please drive slow.
   For this body you are hauling,
   Lord, I hate to see her go."
   Will the circle be unbroken,
   By and by, Lord, by and by?
   There's a better home awaiting,
   In the sky, in the sky.

3. I will follow close behind her,
   Try to hold up and be brave.
   But I could not hide my sorrow,
   When they laid her in her grave.
   Will the circle be unbroken,
   By and by, Lord, by and by?
   There's a better home awaiting,
   In the sky, in the sky.

Scarborough Fair

Traditional English

Lyrics

1. Are you going to Scarborough Fair?
   Parsley, sage, rosemary and thyme.
   Remember me to one who lives there,
   For once he was a true love of mine.

2. Have him make me a cambric shirt,
   Parsley, sage, rosemary and thyme.
   Without a seam or fine needlework,
   And then he'll be a true love of mine.

3. Have him wash it in yonder dry well,
   Parsley, sage, rosemary and thyme.
   Where ne'er a drop of fine water e'er fell,
   And then he'll be a true love of mine.

4. Have him find me an acre of land,
   Parsley, sage, rosemary and thyme.
   Between the sea and over the sand,
   And then he'll be a true love of mine.

5. Plow the land with the horn of a lamb,
   Parsley, sage, rosemary and thyme.
   Then sow some seeds from north of the dam,
   And then he'll be a true love of mine.

6. If he tells me he can't I'll reply:
   Parsley, sage, rosemary and thyme.
   Let me know that at least he will try,
   And then he'll be a true love of mine.

HAL•LEONARD INSTRUMENTAL PLAY-ALONG

Your favorite songs are arranged just for solo instrumentalists with this outstanding series. Each book includes a great full-accompaniment play-along CD so you can sound just like a pro! Check out **www.halleonard.com** to see all the titles available.

Disney Greats

Arabian Nights • Hawaiian Roller Coaster Ride • It's a Small World • Look Through My Eyes • Yo Ho (A Pirate's Life for Me) • and more.

_____	00841934	Flute	$12.95
_____	00841935	Clarinet	$12.95
_____	00841936	Alto Sax	$12.95
_____	00841937	Tenor Sax	$12.95
_____	00841938	Trumpet	$12.95
_____	00841939	Horn	$12.95
_____	00841940	Trombone	$12.95
_____	00841941	Violin	$12.95
_____	00841942	Viola	$12.95
_____	00841943	Cello	$12.95
_____	00842078	Oboe	$12.95

Glee

And I Am Telling You I'm Not Going • Defying Gravity • Don't Stop Believin' • Keep Holding On • Lean on Me • No Air • Sweet Caroline • True Colors • and more.

_____	00842479	Flute	$12.99
_____	00842480	Clarinet	$12.99
_____	00842481	Alto Sax	$12.99
_____	00842482	Tenor Sax	$12.99
_____	00842483	Trumpet	$12.99
_____	00842484	Horn	$12.99
_____	00842485	Trombone	$12.99
_____	00842486	Violin	$12.99
_____	00842487	Viola	$12.99
_____	00842488	Cello	$12.99

Movie Music

And All That Jazz • Come What May • I Am a Man of Constant Sorrow • I Walk the Line • Seasons of Love • Theme from Spider Man • and more.

_____	00842089	Flute	$10.95
_____	00842090	Clarinet	$10.95
_____	00842091	Alto Sax	$10.95
_____	00842092	Tenor Sax	$10.95
_____	00842093	Trumpet	$10.95
_____	00842094	Horn	$10.95
_____	00842095	Trombone	$10.95
_____	00842096	Violin	$10.95
_____	00842097	Viola	$10.95
_____	00842098	Cello	$10.95

Elvis Presley

All Shook Up • Blue Suede Shoes • Can't Help Falling in Love • Don't Be Cruel • Hound Dog • Jailhouse Rock • Love Me Tender • Return to Sender • and more.

_____	00842363	Flute	$12.99
_____	00842367	Trumpet	$12.99
_____	00842368	Horn	$12.99
_____	00842369	Trombone	$12.99
_____	00842370	Violin	$12.99
_____	00842371	Viola	$12.99
_____	00842372	Cello	$12.99

Sports Rock

Another One Bites the Dust • Centerfold • Crazy Train • Get Down Tonight • Let's Get It Started • Shout • The Way You Move • and more.

_____	00842326	Flute	$12.99
_____	00842327	Clarinet	$12.99
_____	00842328	Alto Sax	$12.99
_____	00842329	Tenor Sax	$12.99
_____	00842330	Trumpet	$12.99
_____	00842331	Horn	$12.99
_____	00842332	Trombone	$12.99
_____	00842333	Violin	$12.99
_____	00842334	Viola	$12.99
_____	00842335	Cello	$12.99

TV Favorites

The Addams Family Theme • The Brady Bunch • Green Acres Theme • Happy Days • Johnny's Theme • Linus and Lucy • NFL on Fox Theme • Theme from the Simpsons • and more.

_____	00842079	Flute	$10.95
_____	00842080	Clarinet	$10.95
_____	00842081	Alto Sax	$10.95
_____	00842082	Tenor Sax	$10.95
_____	00842083	Trumpet	$10.95
_____	00842084	Horn	$10.95
_____	00842085	Trombone	$10.95
_____	00842086	Violin	$10.95
_____	00842087	Viola	$10.95
_____	00842088	Cello	$10.95

Twilight

Bella's Lullaby • Decode • Eyes on Fire • Full Moon • Go All the Way (Into the Twilight) • Leave Out All the Rest • Spotlight (Twilight Remix) • Supermassive Black Hole • Tremble for My Beloved.

_____	00842406	Flute	$12.99
_____	00842407	Clarinet	$12.99
_____	00842408	Alto Sax	$12.99
_____	00842409	Tenor Sax	$12.99
_____	00842410	Trumpet	$12.99
_____	00842411	Horn	$12.99
_____	00842412	Trombone	$12.99
_____	00842413	Violin	$12.99
_____	00842414	Viola	$12.99
_____	00842415	Cello	$12.99

Twilight – New Moon

Almost a Kiss • Dreamcatcher • Edward Leaves • I Need You • Memories of Edward • New Moon • Possibility • Roslyn • Satellite Heart • and more.

_____	00842458	Flute	$12.99
_____	00842459	Clarinet	$12.99
_____	00842460	Alto Sax	$12.99
_____	00842461	Tenor Sax	$12.99
_____	00842462	Trumpet	$12.99
_____	00842463	Horn	$12.99
_____	00842464	Trombone	$12.99
_____	00842465	Violin	$12.99
_____	00842466	Viola	$12.99
_____	00842467	Cello	$12.99

Wicked

As Long As You're Mine • Dancing Through Life • Defying Gravity • For Good • I'm Not That Girl • Popular • The Wizard and I • and more.

_____	00842236	Book/CD Pack	$11.95
_____	00842237	Book/CD Pack	$11.95
_____	00842238	Alto Saxophone	$11.95
_____	00842239	Tenor Saxophone	$11.95
_____	00842240	Trumpet	$11.95
_____	00842241	Horn	$11.95
_____	00842242	Trombone	$11.95
_____	00842243	Violin	$11.95
_____	00842244	Viola	$11.95
_____	00842245	Cello	$11.95

FOR MORE INFORMATION, SEE YOUR LOCAL MUSIC DEALER, OR WRITE TO:

HAL•LEONARD® CORPORATION
7777 W. BLUEMOUND RD. P.O. BOX 13819 MILWAUKEE, WI 53213